# Kakuro

# Kakuro

## BOOK 1

First published in Great Britain in 2005 by Virgin Books
Virgin Books Ltd
Thames Wharf Studios
Rainville Road
London
W6 9HA

All puzzles copyright © Nikoli 2005
supplied under license by Puzzler Media Ltd. RH1 1EY
www.puzzler.co.uk

All other material © Virgin Books 2005

A catalogue record for this book is available from the British Library.

ISBN 0-7535-1161-4

The paper used in this book is a natural, recyclable product made
from wood grown in sustainable forests. The manufacturing process
conforms to the regulations of the country of origin.

Typeset by seagulls

Printed and bound in the USA

# INTRODUCTION

Kakuro, the new puzzle craze, is not actually that new – in fact it is probably one of the puzzle world's best kept secrets. Originally published in the late-60s in America, cross sums, as they were then known, were sandwiched neatly inside books of regular crosswords, presumably to give the reader a break from cryptic clues. There they might have stayed, had it not been for McKee Kaji, a Japanese businessman, who chanced upon the puzzles and saw their huge potential ...

Adapting them for his homeland, Kaji redesigned and renamed them 'kasan kurosu', which conjoins the Japanese word for addictive and the pronunciation of the English word 'cross'. Over the years, Kakuro became increasingly popular, so much so that in 1986 Nikoli, Kaji's company and the premier publisher of puzzle books in Japan, issued the first book devoted to Kakuro puzzles. It was an immediate success and over twenty volumes have followed, with sales in excess of a million copies.

So how do you play Kakuro? Just like Su Doku, Kakuro is essentially a logic puzzle – all puzzles in this volume can be solved without the infuriating need to guess and hope – but it adds an element of basic mathematics. The full rules and an explanation of how to play follows this introduction, but, in short, the object of Kakuro is to make each cell of each grid add up to the number attached to it, using only the numbers from one to nine. Those that start to shake at the mere mention of adding up, don't panic. There are only a limited amount of combinations (many of which are listed at the back of the book) that will lead you to a cell's value, for example, if your cell is two squares across and the number beside it is 17, then the only possible combination is 9 and 8. The puzzle is simplicity itself, and takes no time to learn; however, to master it takes patience, thought and an industrial size pencil eraser.

In Japan, Kakuro is so popular that it has overshadowed Su Doku. Why? Well it's a combination of various reasons. The puzzles are more challenging than Su Doku, with a greater variety of grids and more fiendish ways of bamboozling you. It is this variation that hooks the puzzler, that and the tremendous feeling of accomplishment when you complete a grid. The addition of mathematics is also a factor, in that you very quickly pick up on the fact that certain numbers attached to cells with a certain amount of squares only has one possible combination – for example, if a cell has three squares and the number attached to it is 7, then the only combination is 4, 2 and 1. It is amazing how this knowledge becomes automatic and helps you solve puzzles significantly more quickly. As a by-product, it also sharpens your mental arithmetic, which if you considered yourself a mathematical dunce is an unusual and edifying experience.

If this is your first foray into the compulsively addictive world of Kakuro, or you have jumped ship from Su Doku, you will find a huge amount to enjoy within these pages. The book is divided into three sections, increasing in the amount of time it should take you to complete them – bear in mind, therefore, that the ones at the back of the book might take rather longer than your lunch break …

*The Virgin Book of Kakuro* is wickedly addictive and devilish good fun. Enjoy!

# THE RULES

The object of Kakuro is to fill the white squares in the grid, only using numbers between 1 and 9.

Each Kakuro puzzle is made up of cells, which either run up or down, much like a crossword clue. Each cell is made up of between 2 and 9 squares.

These cells must be filled in with numbers that add up to the number 'clue', which is found in the shaded box alongside the cell. If a number appears in the bottom half of the box it is a downwards clue; if in the top half an across clue.

No number can appear twice in a cell.

# HOW TO SOLVE
# A KAKURO PUZZLE

## STEP ONE

It is helpful to look for cells with the fewest squares, as these tend to be the easiest to solve. In this case there are several cells with just two squares.

A good place to start is on the right-hand side where there are two cells together with just two squares. These are marked with question marks below:

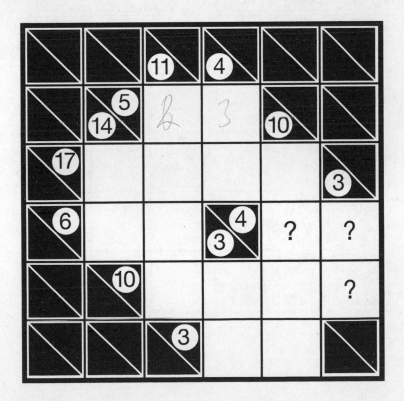

The cell running across, which must add up to **4**, can only contain 1 and 3 as no cell can have the same number twice.

The downwards cell that it joins adds up to **3**, which means the only possible combination is 1 and 2.

This therefore means that we know that the 1 must appear on both the **3** down cell and the **4** across cell. The puzzle now looks like this:

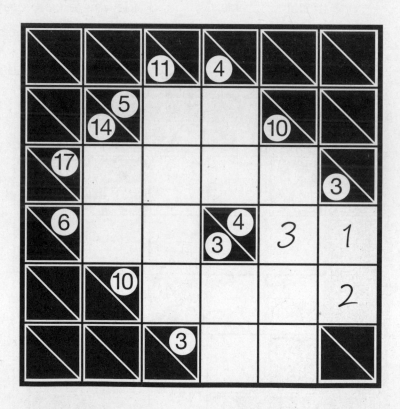

## STEP TWO

There is now a 2 on the cell running across marked with **10**.

Two squares to the left of this 2 there is a downwards cell that is marked with **3**.

Because we can't have the same number on that line, and the only combination for 3 is 2+1, we can deduce that this square must be filled with a 1.

The across cell beneath it, also marked with **3**, must therefore be filled in with a 2 then a 1, as below:

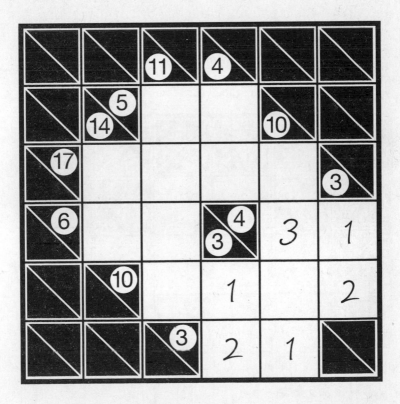

## STEP THREE

We now have a 1 and a 2 on the **10** across cell. This means that the remaining squares must add up to 7.

In this case 7 has three possible combinations: 5+2, 1+6 and 3+4. As there is already a 1 and a 2 in the cell, the only possible combination is 3+4

As the blank square between the 1 and the 2 is also on another cell (the **10** down cell), which already contains a 3, we know that this is where the 4 must go and can add the 3 to the final remaining square.

With the **10** across line now filled, we can also complete the **10** down clue (3+1+4=8, therefore the last blank square must be a 2). As below:

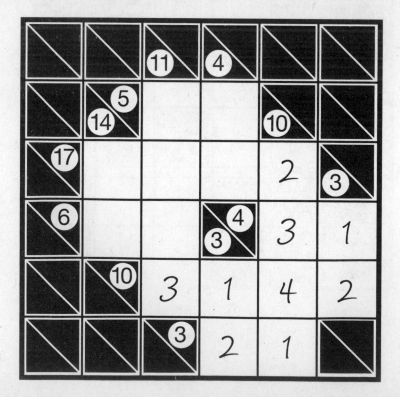

## STEP FOUR

On the left-hand side of the puzzle is another pair of cells that have two spaces, one marked **14** going down and one marked **6** going across.

The only combinations for **14** are 8+6 and 9+5. However, as the cell below must add up to **6**, the only legal move is 9+5 running downwards, as all the other numbers would make the sum too high. This makes the **6** across cell 5+1 as below:

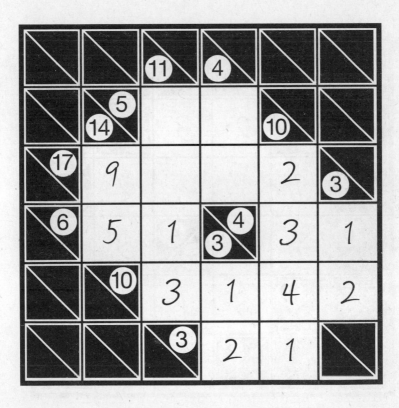

## STEP FIVE

The cell across the top of puzzle adds up to **5**, which has only two combinations 1+4 and 2+3.

As 1 and 3 already appear on the cell running downwards marked with **11**, the left-hand square can only be a 2 or a 4.

However, if it was a 4 then the missing digit on the **11** down cell would have to be a 3, which is already represented. Therefore the **5** across cell must be 2+3 as below:

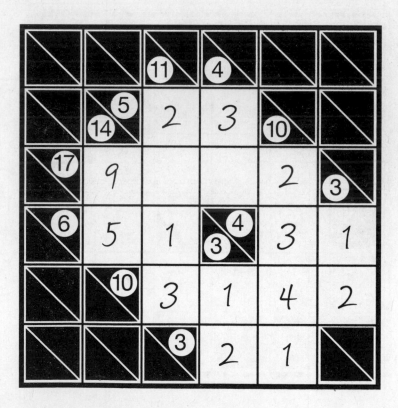

## FINAL STEP

The puzzle is now easily solved by adding the 1 to make up the **4** down cell and a 5 to complete the **17** across/**11** down cell.

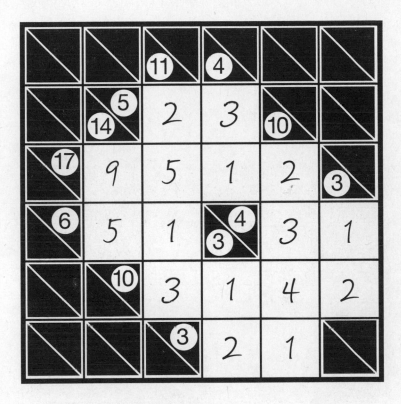

# Easy
# Puzzles

# EASY PUZZLES
## 1

*See page 125 for the solution*

*See page 125 for the solution*

*See page 125 for the solution*

*See page 125 for the solution*

*See page 125 for the solution*

# 6

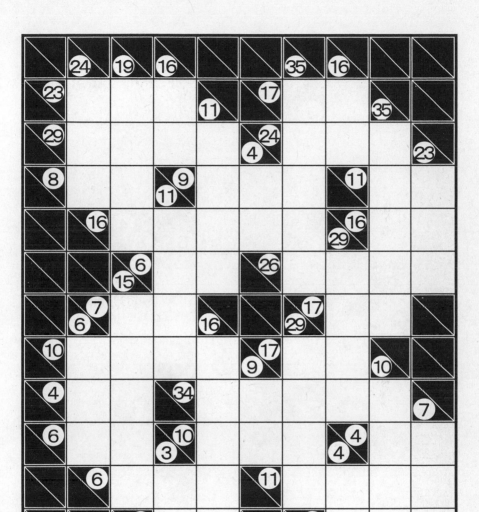

*See page 125 for the solution*

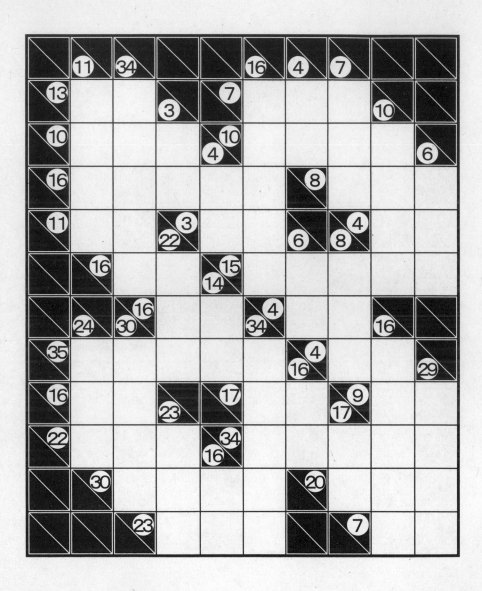

*See page 126 for the solution*

*See page 126 for the solution*

*See page 126 for the solution*

*See page 126 for the solution*

## 11

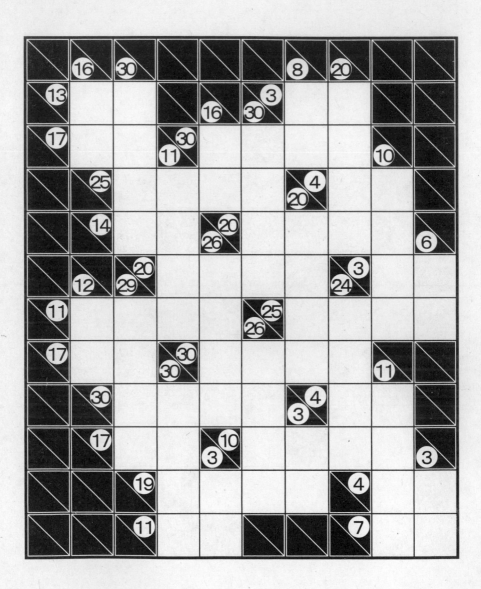

*See page 126 for the solution*

*See page 126 for the solution*

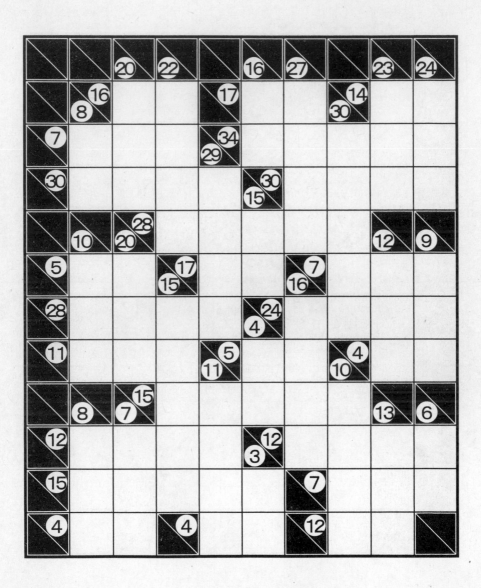

*See page 126 for the solution*

*See page 126 for the solution*

*See page 127 for the solution*

*See page 127 for the solution*

*See page 127 for the solution*

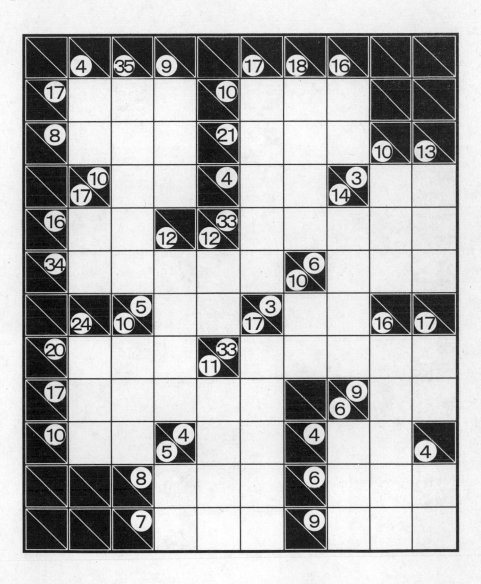

*See page 127 for the solution*

*See page 127 for the solution*

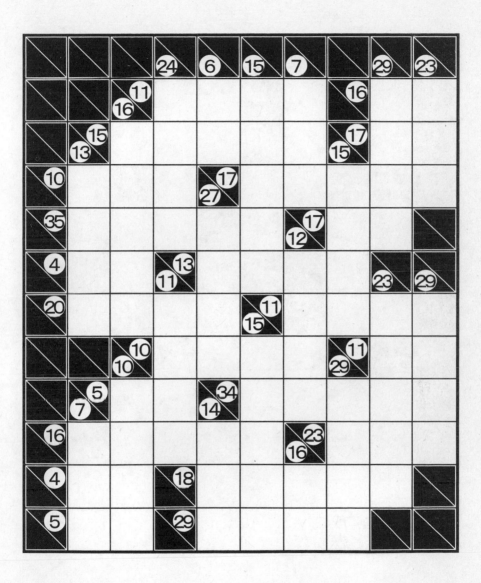

*See page 127 for the solution*

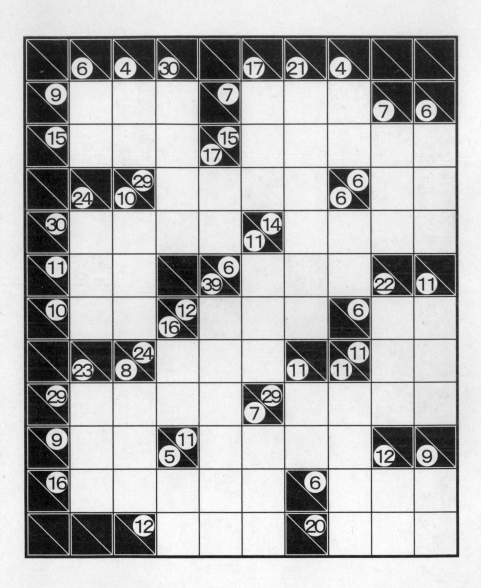

*See page 127 for the solution*

*See page 127 for the solution*

*See page 128 for the solution*

*See page 128 for the solution*

*See page 128 for the solution*

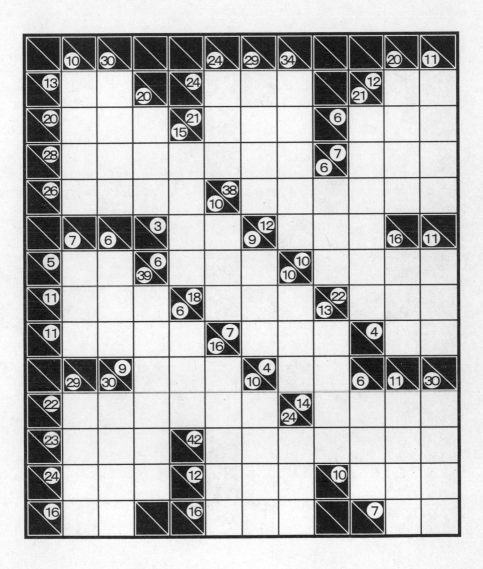

*See page 128 for the solution*

*See page 128 for the solution*

*See page 128 for the solution*

*See page 128 for the solution*

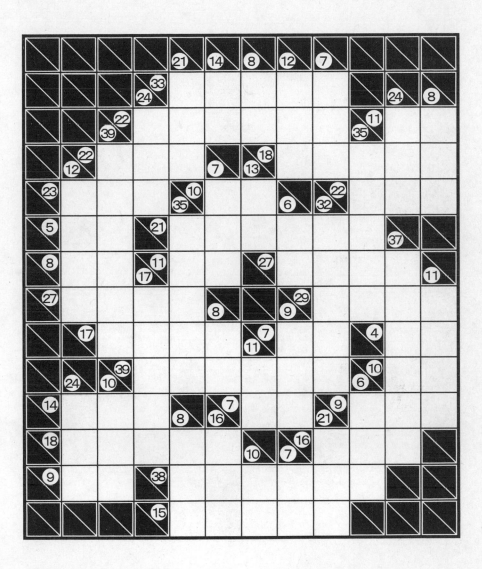

*See page 128 for the solution*

## 31

*See page 129 for the solution*

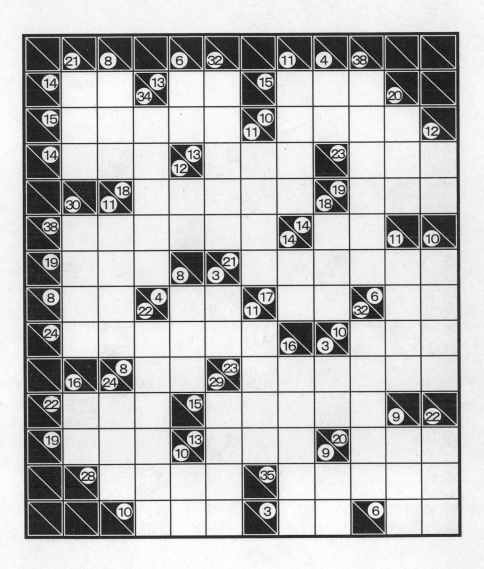

*See page 129 for the solution*

*See page 129 for the solution*

*See page 129 for the solution*

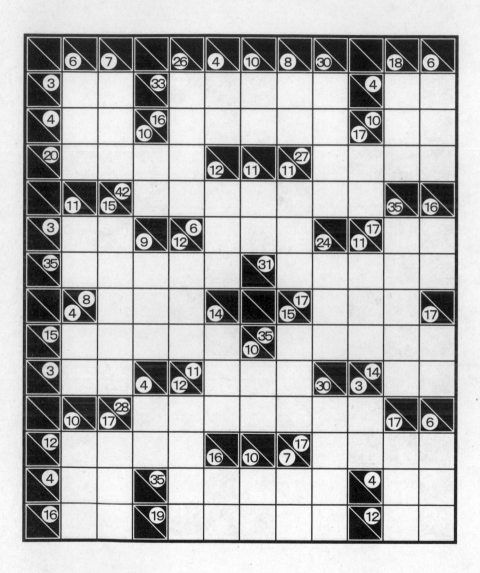

*See page 129 for the solution*

*See page 129 for the solution*

*See page 129 for the solution*

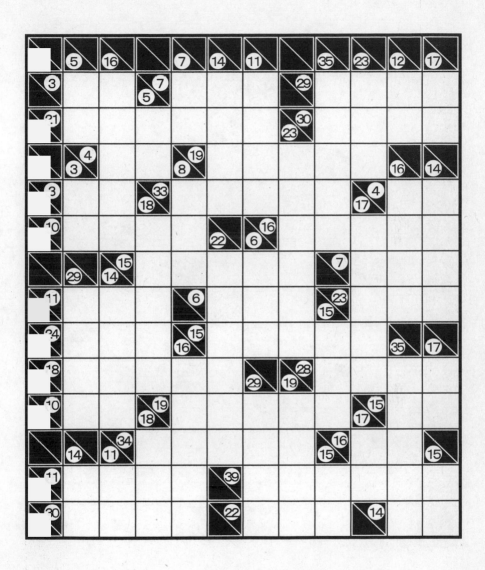

*See page 129 for the solution*

*See page 130 for the solution*

*See page 130 for the solution*

*See page 130 for the solution*

*See page 130 for the solution*

*See page 130 for the solution*

*See page 130 for the solution*

*See page 130 for the solution*

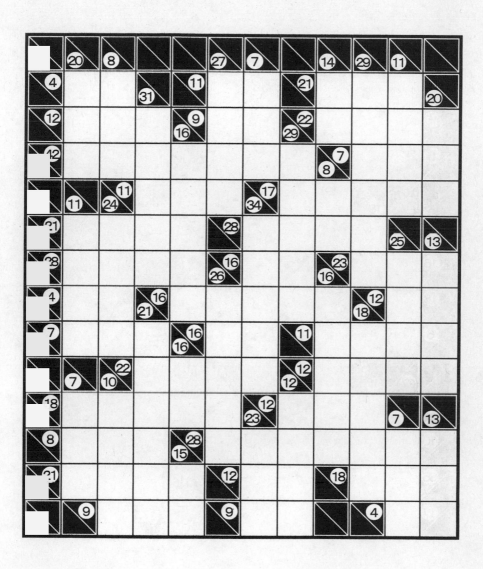

*See page 130 for the solution*

*See page 131 for the solution*

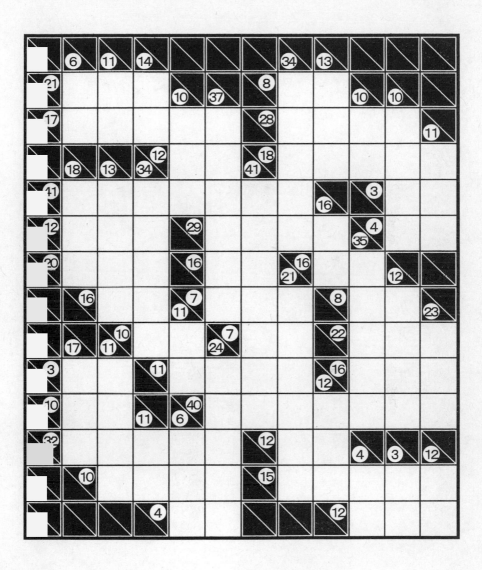

*See page 131 for the solution*

## 49

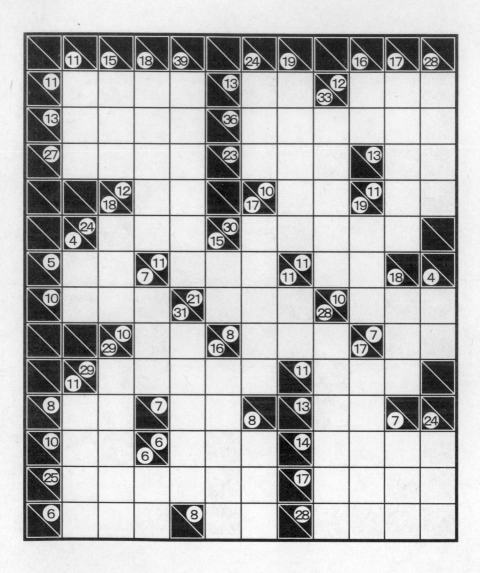

*See page 131 for the solution*

*See page 131 for the solution*

# Medium Puzzles

## 51

*See page 131 for the solution*

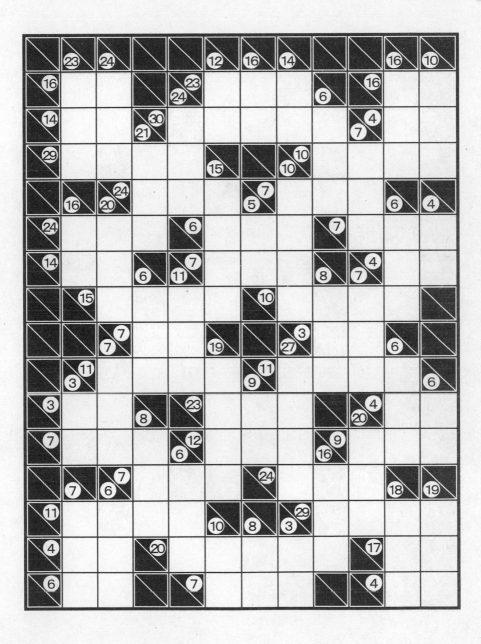

*See page 131 for the solution*

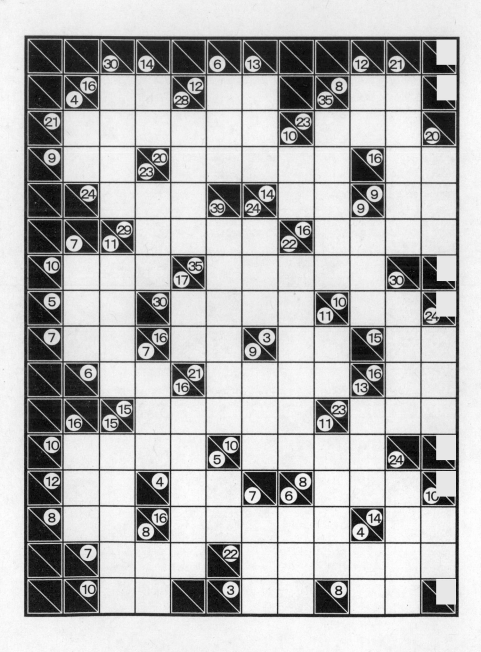

*See page 132 for the solution*

*See page 132 for the solution*

*See page 132 for the solution*

*See page 132 for the solution*

# 57

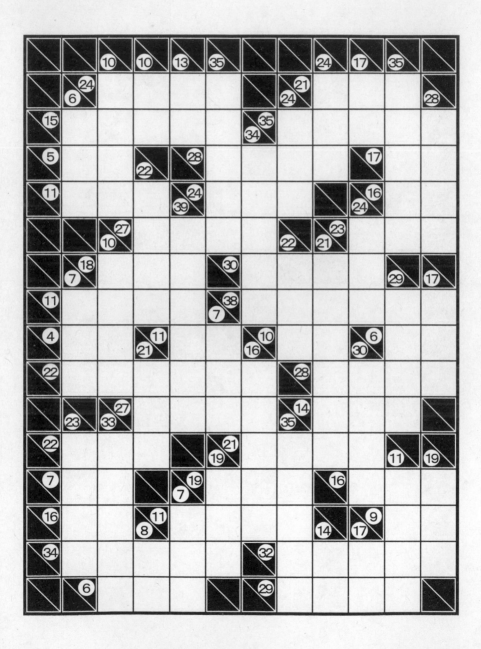

*See page 132 for the solution*

*See page 132 for the solution*

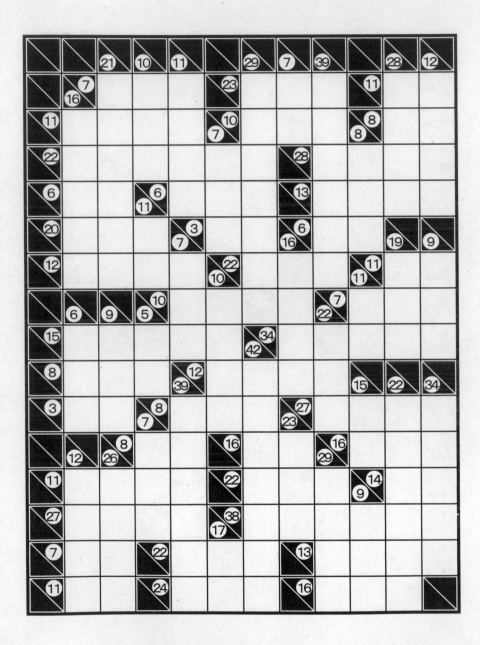

*See page 133 for the solution*

*See page 133 for the solution*

## 61

*See page 133 for the solution*

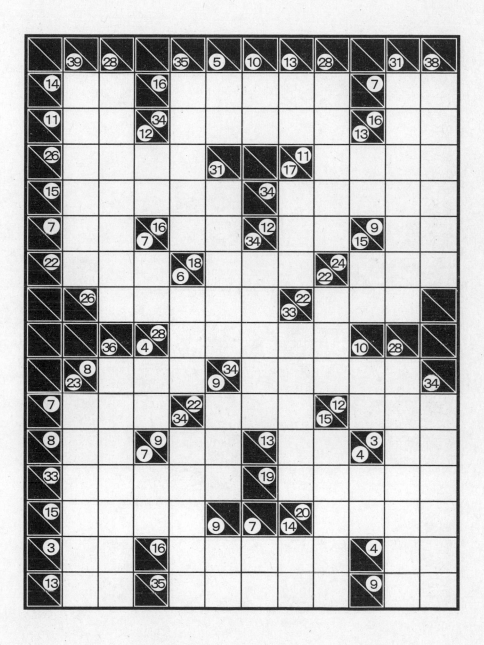

*See page 133 for the solution*

# 63

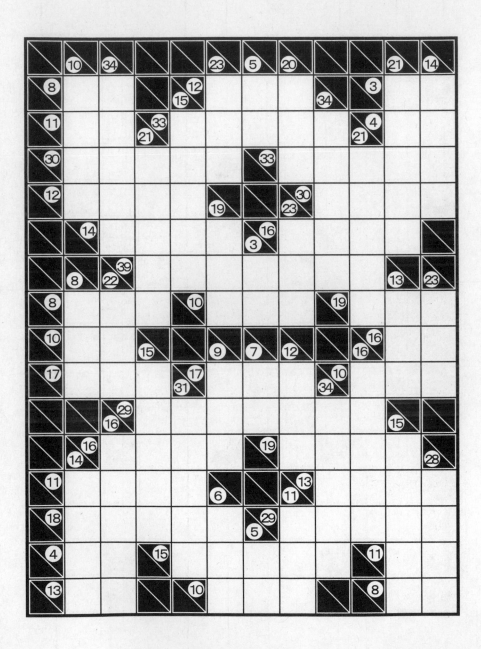

*See page 133 for the solution*

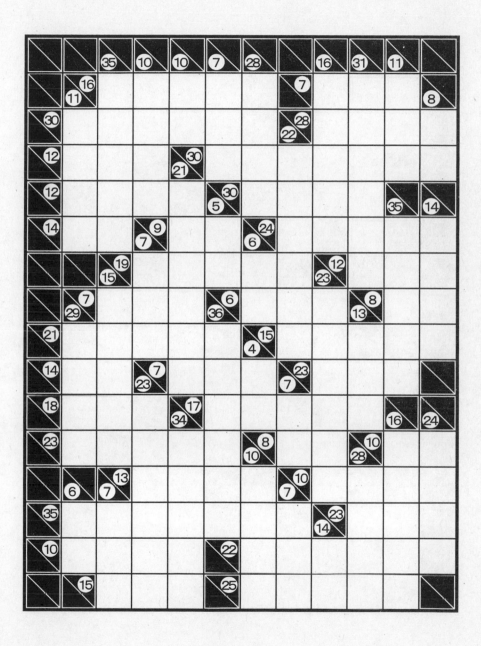

*See page 133 for the solution*

# 65

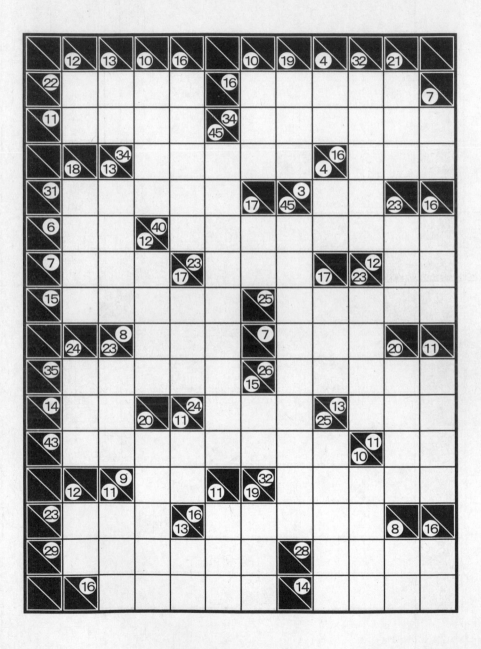

*See page 134 for the solution*

*See page 134 for the solution*

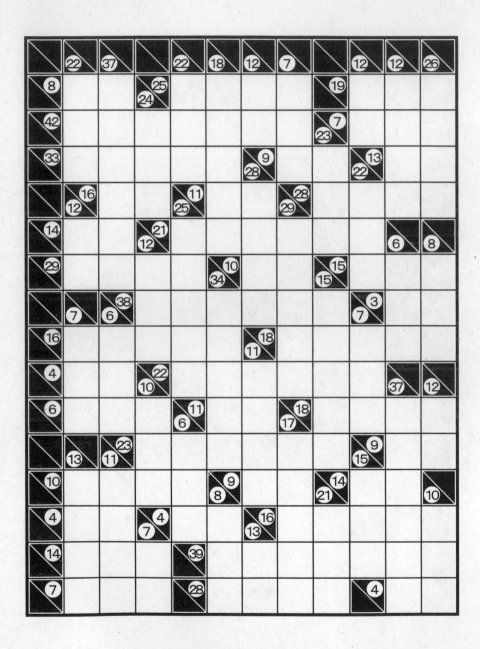

*See page 134 for the solution*

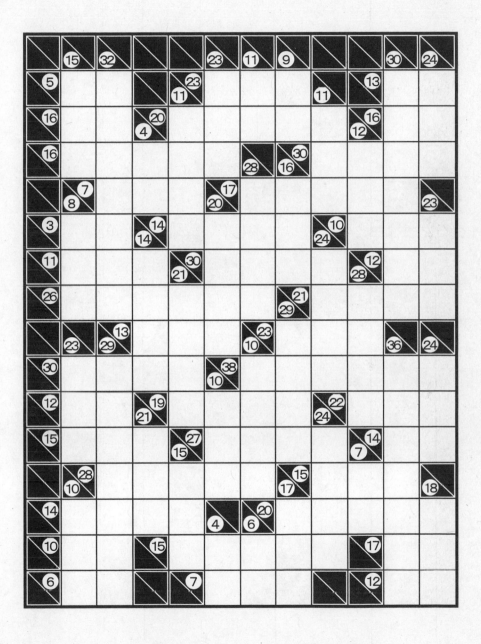

*See page 134 for the solution*

# 69

*See page 134 for the solution*

*See page 134 for the solution*

*See page 135 for the solution*

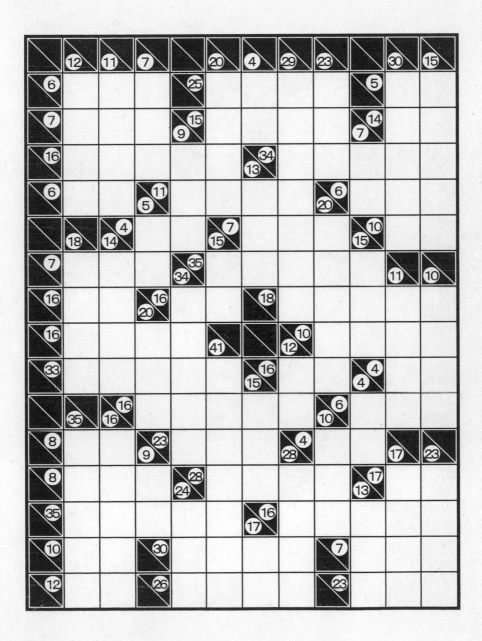

*See page 135 for the solution*

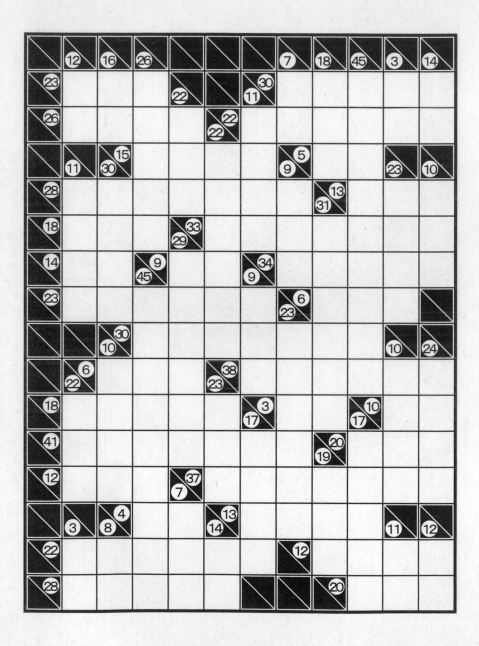

*See page 135 for the solution*

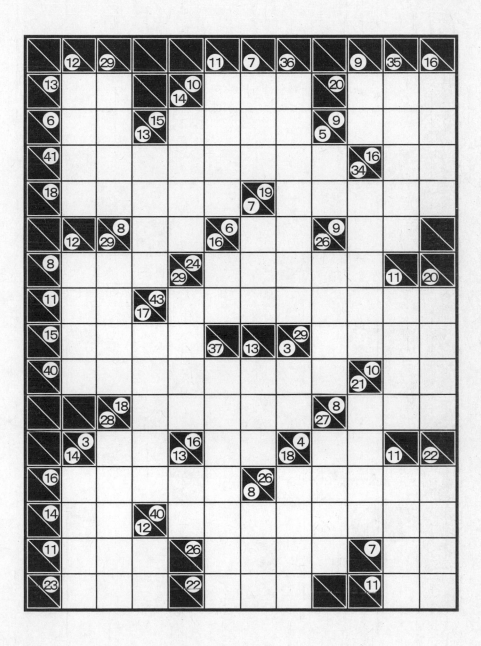

*See page 135 for the solution*

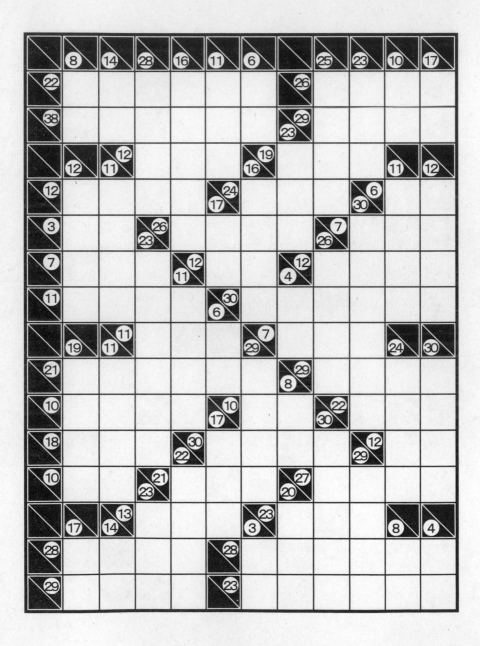

*See page 135 for the solution*

*See page 135 for the solution*

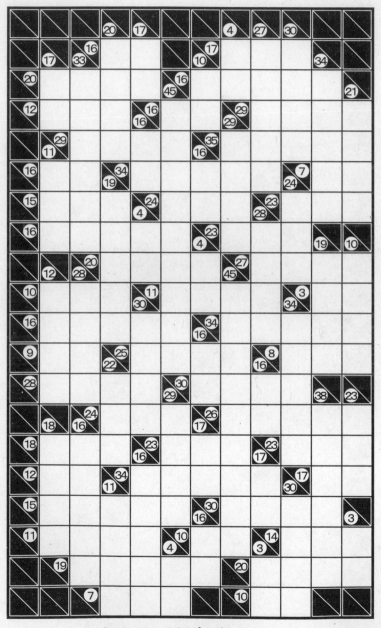

*See page 136 for the solution*

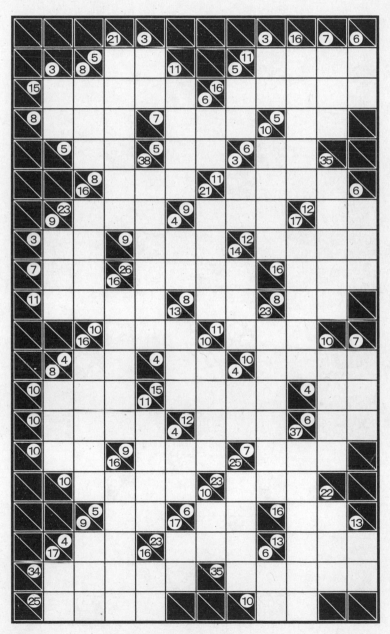

*See page 136 for the solution*

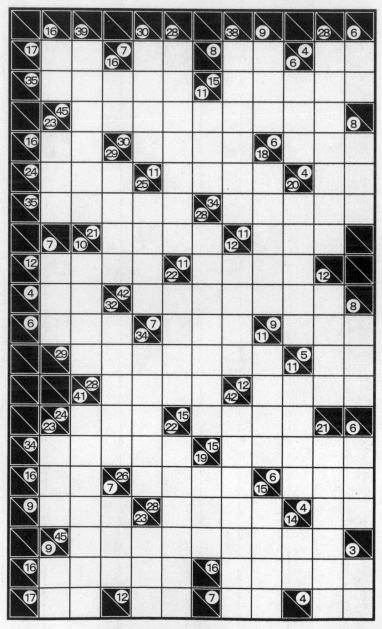

*See page 136 for the solution*

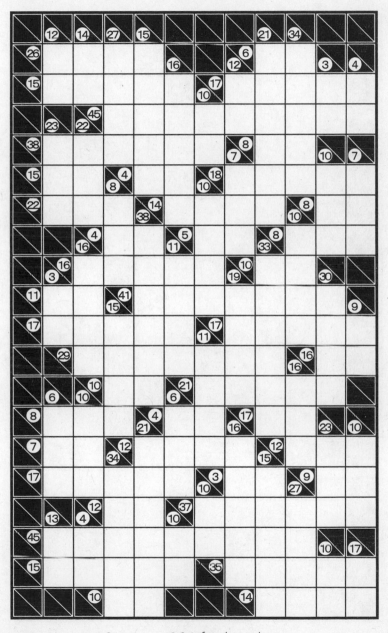

*See page 136 for the solution*

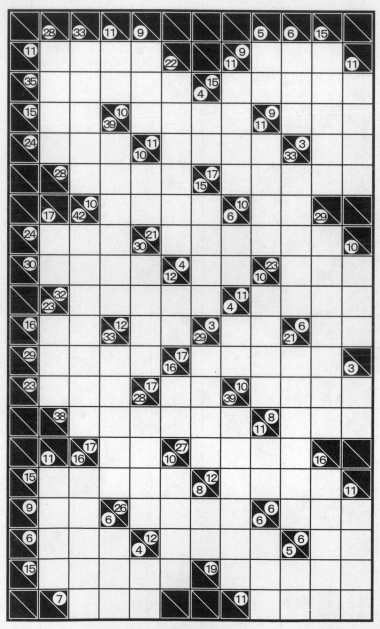

*See page 136 for the solution*

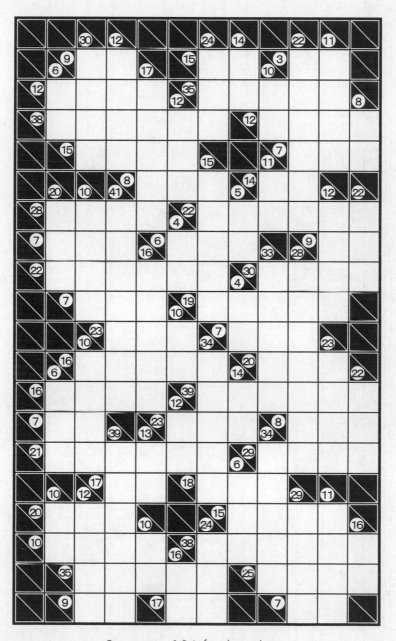

*See page 136 for the solution*

## 83

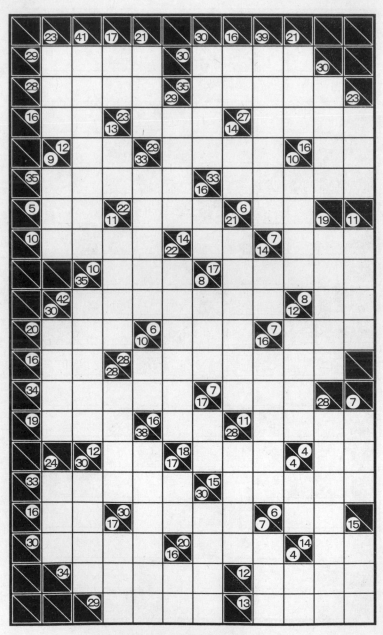

*See page 137 for the solution*

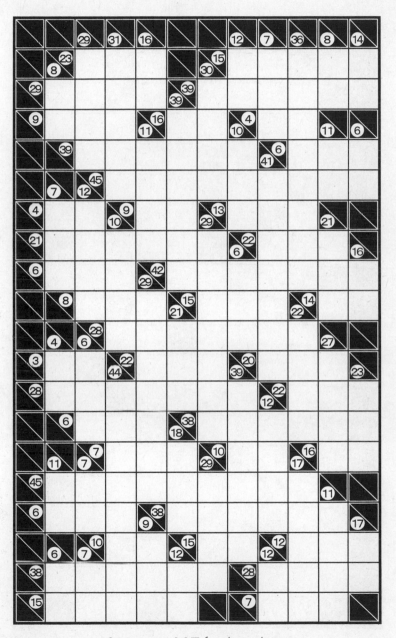

*See page 137 for the solution*

# 85

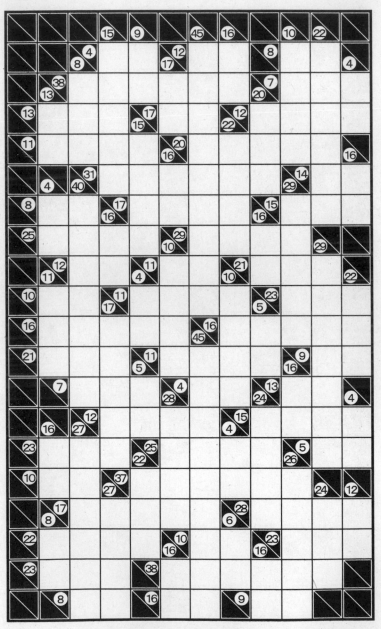

*See page 137 for the solution*

*See page 137 for the solution*

## 87

*See page 137 for the solution*

*See page 137 for the solution*

# 89

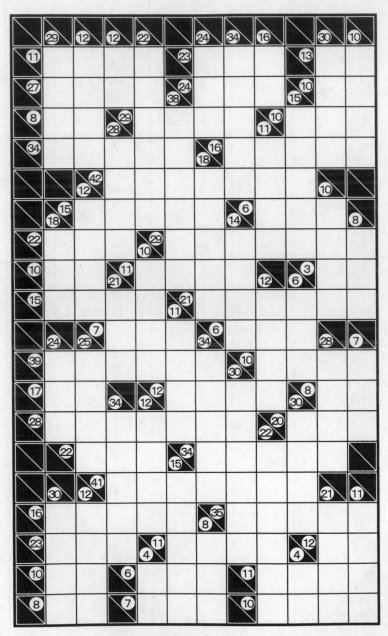

*See page 138 for the solution*

*See page 138 for the solution*

# Hard
# Puzzles

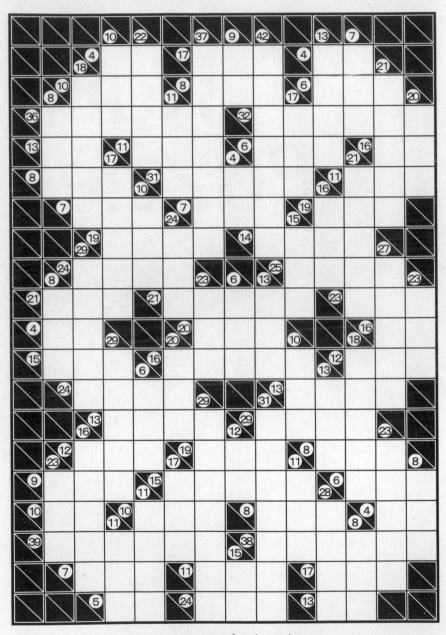

*See page 138 for the solution*

*See page 138 for the solution*

*See page 138 for the solution*

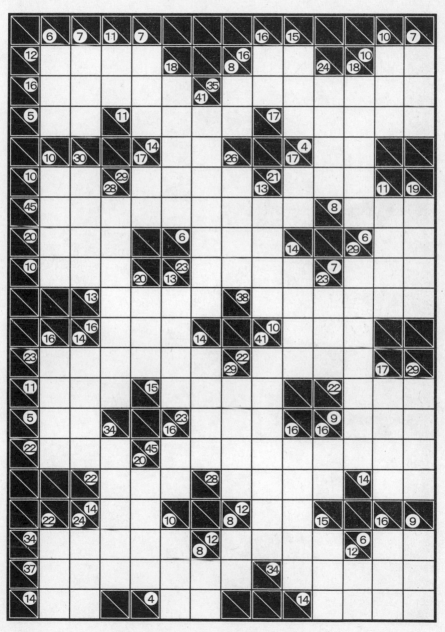

*See page 138 for the solution*

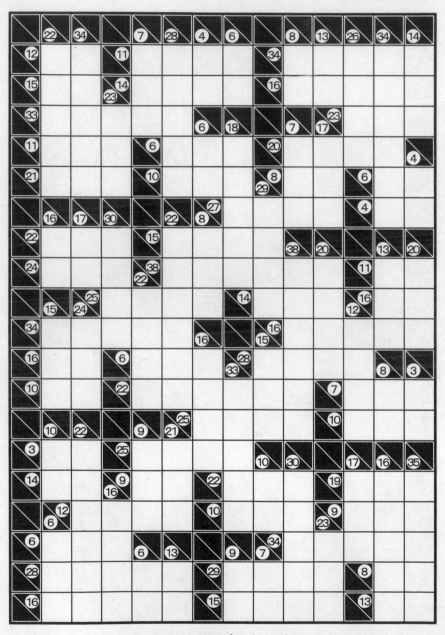

*See page 139 for the solution*

*See page 139 for the solution*

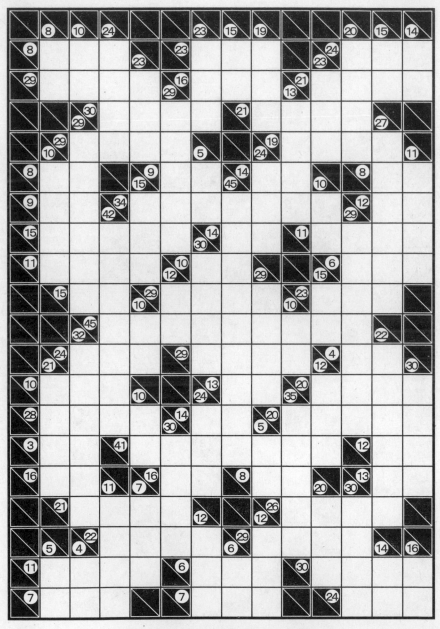

*See page 139 for the solution*

*See page 139 for the solution*

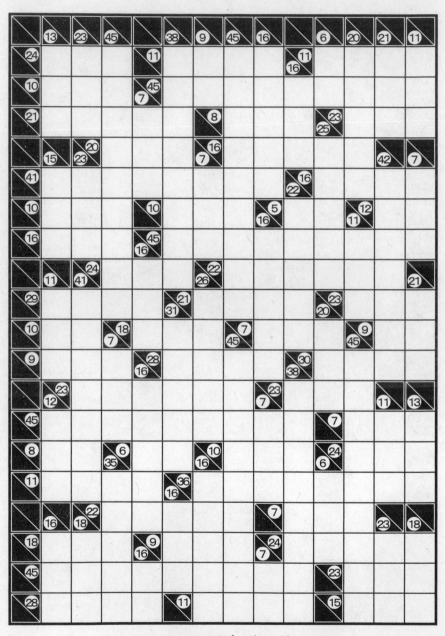

*See page 139 for the solution*

*See page 142 for the competition!*

# LIST OF UNIQUE NUMBER COMBINATIONS

This list helps you identify where there is only one possibility to a cell's value – invaluable to helping you solve a Kakuro.

**2 Cells**
3  : 1,2
4  : 1,3
16: 9,7
17: 9,8

**3 Cells**
6  : 1,2,3
7  : 1,2,4
23: 6,8,9
24: 7,8,9

**4 Cells**
10: 1,2,3,4
11: 1,2,3,5
29: 5,7,8,9
30: 6,7,8,9

**5 Cells**
15: 1,2,3,4,5
16: 1,2,3,4,6
34: 4,6,7,8,9
35: 5,6,7,8,9

**6 Cells**
21: 1,2,3,4,5,6
22: 1,2,3,4,5,7
38: 3,5,6,7,8,9
39: 4,5,6,7,8,9

**7 Cells**
28: 1,2,3,4,5,6,7
29: 1,2,3,4,5,6,8
41: 2,4,5,6,7,8,9
42: 3,4,5,6,7,8,9

**8 Cells**
36: 1,2,3,4,5,6,7,8
37: 1,2,3,4,5,6,7,9
38: 1,2,3,4,5,6,8,9
39: 1,2,3,4,5,7,8,9
40: 1,2,3,4,6,7,8,9
41: 1,2,3,5,6,7,8,9
42: 1,2,4,5,6,7,8,9
43: 1,3,4,5,6,7,8,9
44: 2,3,4,5,6,7,8,9

**9 Cells**
45: 1,2,3,4,5,6,7,8,9

# ANSWERS

EASY **1**

EASY **2**

EASY **3**

EASY **4**

EASY **5**

EASY **6**

## EASY 7

| 5 | 8 |   |   | 4 | 1 | 2 |   |   |
| 3 | 6 | 1 |   | 1 | 3 | 4 | 2 |   |
| 1 | 4 | 2 | 3 | 6 |   | 1 | 4 | 3 |
| 2 | 9 |   | 1 | 2 |   |   | 3 | 1 |
|   | 7 | 9 |   | 3 | 5 | 4 | 1 | 2 |
|   |   | 7 | 9 |   | 1 | 3 |   |   |
| 8 | 9 | 6 | 5 | 7 |   | 1 | 3 |   |
| 9 | 7 |   |   | 8 | 9 |   | 1 | 8 |
| 7 | 6 | 9 |   | 4 | 7 | 8 | 6 | 9 |
|   | 8 | 6 | 7 | 9 |   | 9 | 4 | 7 |
|   |   | 8 | 9 | 6 |   |   | 2 | 5 |

## EASY 8

| 1 | 4 |   | 7 | 8 | 9 |   | 2 | 8 |
| 3 | 1 |   | 9 | 6 | 8 |   | 7 | 9 |
| 5 | 2 | 1 | 3 |   | 6 | 8 | 1 | 7 |
|   |   |   | 4 | 8 |   | 7 | 9 |   |
| 8 | 6 | 2 | 5 |   | 3 | 6 | 1 | 2 |
| 9 | 7 |   |   |   |   |   | 3 | 1 |
| 6 | 9 | 5 | 8 |   | 5 | 8 | 9 | 7 |
|   |   | 1 | 6 |   | 4 | 9 |   |   |
| 6 | 8 | 9 | 7 |   | 3 | 6 | 2 | 1 |
| 1 | 9 |   | 9 | 3 | 1 |   | 1 | 3 |
| 2 | 6 |   | 3 | 1 | 2 |   | 5 | 9 |

## EASY 9

| 3 | 4 |   | 5 | 1 |   | 6 | 8 |   |
| 1 | 5 | 4 | 2 | 3 |   | 2 | 7 | 1 |
|   | 3 | 2 | 1 |   | 1 | 3 | 5 | 2 |
| 1 | 2 |   | 3 | 1 | 9 |   | 6 | 4 |
| 3 | 1 | 2 |   | 7 | 8 | 4 | 9 |   |
|   |   | 4 | 2 |   | 2 | 1 |   |   |
|   | 2 | 1 | 5 | 3 |   | 2 | 4 | 1 |
| 2 | 1 |   | 3 | 2 | 1 |   | 2 | 3 |
| 3 | 4 | 2 | 1 |   | 2 | 5 | 8 |   |
| 1 | 6 | 3 |   | 6 | 4 | 7 | 9 | 8 |
|   | 3 | 1 |   | 2 | 3 |   | 7 | 9 |

## EASY 10

| 2 | 7 | 6 |   | 3 | 1 | 2 | 4 |
| 6 | 9 | 8 |   | 9 | 7 | 6 | 5 | 8 |
|   |   | 7 | 9 | 6 | 8 |   | 3 | 1 |
|   | 7 | 9 | 5 | 8 |   | 8 | 1 |   |
| 1 | 3 |   | 8 | 7 | 3 | 9 |   |   |
| 2 | 1 | 4 | 3 |   | 7 | 6 | 9 | 8 |
|   | 2 | 7 | 3 | 1 |   | 7 | 9 |   |
|   | 3 | 1 |   | 9 | 4 | 7 | 8 |   |
| 9 | 2 |   | 3 | 5 | 2 | 1 |   |   |
| 8 | 5 | 9 | 1 | 2 |   | 9 | 1 | 3 |
| 3 | 1 | 5 | 2 |   |   | 2 | 4 | 1 |

## EASY 11

| 7 | 6 |   |   |   | 2 | 1 |   |   |
| 9 | 8 |   | 7 | 8 | 6 | 9 |   |   |
|   | 7 | 3 | 9 | 6 |   | 3 | 1 |   |
|   | 9 | 5 |   | 9 | 1 | 7 | 3 |   |
|   |   | 2 | 8 | 7 | 3 |   | 2 | 1 |
| 3 | 5 | 1 | 2 |   | 7 | 9 | 4 | 5 |
| 9 | 8 |   | 7 | 6 | 9 | 8 |   |   |
|   | 7 | 6 | 9 | 8 |   | 3 | 1 |   |
|   | 9 | 8 |   | 3 | 1 | 4 | 2 |   |
|   | 7 | 1 | 9 | 2 |   | 3 | 1 |   |
|   | 9 | 2 |   |   | 5 | 2 |   |   |

## EASY 12

| 1 | 3 |   |   | 9 | 6 | 8 |   |   |
| 2 | 1 | 3 |   | 7 | 8 | 5 | 6 | 9 |
| 4 | 2 | 1 | 5 | 3 |   | 8 | 9 | 7 |
|   |   | 4 | 3 |   | 5 | 9 |   |   |
| 1 | 4 | 2 |   | 3 | 1 | 7 | 2 | 6 |
| 2 | 5 |   | 3 | 1 | 4 |   | 3 | 4 |
| 3 | 1 | 4 | 2 | 5 |   | 7 | 1 | 2 |
|   |   | 5 | 1 |   | 8 | 9 |   |   |
| 4 | 2 | 1 |   | 6 | 9 | 5 | 8 | 4 |
| 2 | 1 | 6 | 3 | 4 |   | 8 | 6 | 9 |
|   | 4 | 2 | 1 |   |   |   | 9 | 7 |

## EASY 13

|   | 7 | 9 |   | 9 | 8 |   | 6 | 8 |
| 2 | 4 | 1 |   | 7 | 4 | 6 | 8 | 9 |
| 6 | 9 | 8 | 7 |   | 6 | 8 | 9 | 7 |
|   | 4 | 5 | 7 | 9 | 3 |   |   |   |
| 2 | 3 |   | 9 | 8 |   | 4 | 1 | 2 |
| 7 | 9 | 4 | 8 |   | 1 | 9 | 8 | 6 |
| 1 | 8 | 2 |   | 1 | 4 |   | 3 | 1 |
|   |   | 1 | 2 | 3 | 5 | 4 |   |   |
| 4 | 2 | 5 | 1 |   | 6 | 1 | 3 | 2 |
| 1 | 4 | 3 | 5 | 2 |   | 2 | 1 | 4 |
| 3 | 1 |   | 3 | 1 |   | 3 | 9 |   |

## EASY 14

| 1 | 3 |   | 4 | 1 | 5 | 2 |   |   |
| 9 | 4 |   | 8 | 4 | 7 | 6 | 9 |   |
| 4 | 2 | 1 |   | 2 | 8 |   | 4 | 8 |
|   | 6 | 7 | 4 | 8 | 9 |   | 7 | 6 |
|   | 1 | 5 | 2 | 3 |   | 4 | 8 | 9 |
|   | 3 | 1 |   | 1 | 3 |   |   |   |
| 4 | 1 | 2 |   | 1 | 5 | 2 | 4 |   |
| 1 | 3 |   | 9 | 8 | 7 | 6 | 5 |   |
| 3 | 2 |   | 1 | 3 |   | 1 | 2 | 4 |
|   | 5 | 4 | 3 | 2 | 1 |   | 3 | 1 |
|   | 9 | 8 | 4 | 7 |   | 1 | 2 |   |

**EASY 15**

```
1 2 . . 5 2 3 1 .
3 1 6 . 4 5 1 2 3
8 5 9 7 1 . 2 4 1
. . 8 9 . 2 4 . .
8 9 7 . 8 4 6 7 9
6 3 . 7 9 1 . 1 7
9 7 5 8 6 . 7 9 8
. . 1 9 . 7 9 . .
1 2 3 . 5 8 6 9 7
6 7 4 9 8 . 8 6 9
. 1 2 5 3 . 8 2 .
```

**EASY 16**

```
7 9 8 . 8 9 . 8 7
2 7 6 . 9 7 4 6 8
1 3 4 2 7 . 1 3 9
. . 1 3 . 1 2 . .
8 5 3 . 5 2 3 4 1
9 7 . 2 9 3 . 1 3
7 6 9 5 8 . 9 6 2
. . 8 1 . 9 8 . .
8 2 7 . 2 6 5 3 1
7 1 4 8 9 . 6 1 2
9 7 . 2 1 . 7 9 8
```

**EASY 17**

```
. 3 1 9 . . . .
. 1 2 3 7 4 . .
6 2 4 . 9 6 7 8
3 4 . 9 8 3 6 7
6 1 . 7 2 1 . .
2 4 1 . . 2 4 1
. 2 4 1 . 6 2 .
1 2 4 7 3 . 9 7
3 8 7 9 . 1 8 5
. 3 8 1 2 5 . .
. . 3 4 7 . .
```

**EASY 18**

```
3 8 6 . 2 1 7 .
1 5 2 . 4 8 9 .
. 9 1 . 1 3 . 2 1
9 7 . 3 6 8 7 9
8 6 4 9 7 . 2 1 3
. . 2 3 . 2 1 . .
8 7 5 . 7 8 3 6 9
7 2 1 3 4 . 1 8
9 1 . 1 3 . 1 3 .
. 1 5 2 . 3 2 1
. 4 2 1 . 2 4 3
```

**EASY 19**

```
. 2 3 . 9 8 . 9 7
1 4 2 . 7 9 8 6 4
3 1 5 2 . 7 9 8 5
. . 1 3 2 6 4 . .
2 4 . 1 5 . 6 7 9
3 1 2 4 . 3 7 9 8
1 2 4 . 1 2 . 8 6
. . 5 1 3 4 2 . .
4 1 3 2 . 1 5 2 3
6 2 1 4 3 . 3 1 2
9 3 . 5 1 . 1 4 .
```

**EASY 20**

```
. 3 5 1 2 . 7 9 .
. 3 5 1 2 4 . 9 8
1 2 7 . 3 1 2 5 6
7 6 9 8 5 . 9 8 .
3 1 . 6 4 2 1 . .
2 4 5 9 . 1 3 2 5
. 2 4 1 3 . 4 7 .
. 2 3 . 4 6 7 8 9
2 4 1 6 3 . 9 6 8
1 3 . 1 2 7 5 3 .
4 1 . 7 5 9 8 . .
```

**EASY 21**

```
2 1 6 . 4 2 1 . .
4 3 8 . 5 4 3 2 1
. . 7 9 8 5 . 4 2
7 6 9 8 . 6 4 1 3
8 3 . . 1 3 2 . .
9 1 . 9 2 1 . 5 1
. . 9 7 8 . . 8 3
9 5 7 8 . 8 5 9 7
8 1 . 5 2 3 1 . .
6 2 3 4 1 . 2 3 1
. 2 6 4 . 3 9 8 .
```

**EASY 22**

```
9 4 7 8 6 . 6 9 8
4 2 3 5 1 . 9 7 4
. . . 6 9 2 8 7 .
7 5 8 . . 9 8 3 7
8 7 9 6 5 . 4 1 6
5 1 . 2 4 1 . 5 9
6 9 7 . 1 3 4 2 5
9 8 6 7 . . 9 4 8
. . 8 9 1 2 7 . .
2 1 4 . 2 4 6 1 3
8 6 9 . 6 9 8 3 7
```

EASY **23**

EASY **24**

EASY **25**

EASY **26**

EASY **27**

EASY **28**

EASY **29**

EASY **30**

EASY **31**

EASY **32**

EASY **33**

EASY **34**

EASY **35**

EASY **36**

EASY **37**

EASY **38**

# ANSWERS - EASY

EASY **39**

EASY **40**

EASY **41**

EASY **42**

EASY **43**

EASY **44**

EASY **45**

EASY **46**

**EASY 47**

```
5 2 1 . . 9 5 8 . 1 7
9 8 3 1 . 8 1 2 7 5 9
. 9 5 2 1 3 . 1 2 3 6
. 8 3 2 7 1 . 9 4 .
. 2 9 7 4 . 4 2 3 .
1 4 7 . 8 6 . 9 1 8
4 9 . 4 3 1 5 7 . 4 8
. 3 6 1 . 4 6 . 3 1 5
. 9 3 8 . 9 1 5 2 .
. 6 8 . 7 9 8 2 1 .
2 8 7 9 . 8 4 3 2 1
1 4 2 8 9 6 . 6 4 2 1
6 9 . 5 2 1 . 9 5 8
```

**EASY 48**

```
4 8 9 . 6 2 . .
2 3 5 1 6 . 7 8 9 4
. . 4 8 . 4 3 1 2 8
4 2 7 5 9 6 8 . 1 2
5 1 6 . 5 8 9 7 . 3 1
9 3 8 . 7 9 . 9 7 .
. 7 9 . 2 4 1 . 6 2
. . 4 6 . 5 2 . 8 5 9
1 2 . 5 1 2 3 . 9 1 6
7 3 . 9 7 6 1 5 4 8
9 5 8 3 7 . 4 8 .
. 1 3 2 4 . 5 3 1 2 4
. . 1 3 . . 3 1 8
```

**EASY 49**

```
3 2 1 5 . 8 5 . 7 1 4
1 4 2 6 . 7 4 5 9 3 8
7 9 3 8 . 9 6 8 . 6 7
. 5 7 . 1 9 . 2 9
. 8 7 9 . 6 3 7 9 5 .
1 4 . 4 6 1 . 4 7
3 6 1 . 9 5 7 . 3 6 1
. 2 8 . 3 4 1 . 4 3
. 8 4 9 6 2 . 2 1 8
5 3 . 5 2 . 9 4 .
1 9 . 3 1 2 . 3 2 1 8
2 7 5 6 4 1 . 5 3 2 7
3 2 1 . 3 5 . 8 7 4 9
```

**EASY 50**

```
. 2 8 1 4 . 8 9 5 7
8 5 9 3 7 . 6 7 3 8 9
2 1 5 . 5 1 4 . 1 4 8
7 4 . 6 8 5 9 7 . 2 6
9 6 . 1 9 2 7 5 . 3 7
4 3 1 2 6 . 5 2 3 1 4
. 6 8 . . 4 1 .
9 6 7 4 8 . 1 6 2 3 4
2 1 . 3 2 1 7 8 . 4 7
1 3 . 5 6 7 8 9 . 6 9
8 4 9 . 3 2 9 . 3 1 6
6 7 8 9 5 . 6 7 9 5 8
. 2 5 4 1 . 4 1 8 2
```

**MEDIUM 51**

```
1 2 . . 1 4 2 . . 5 9
3 1 2 . 3 1 4 . 9 6 8
. 8 6 7 9 . 3 1 7 2 .
. 1 5 . . 2 8 .
1 5 3 . 4 1 2 . 5 9 7
3 4 . 5 3 1 . 8 9
. 3 7 9 8 . 3 1 5 7
. 4 8 . . 3 4 .
. 4 5 6 9 . 4 2 1 3
9 1 . 2 4 1 . 4 8
8 2 9 . 1 6 3 . 8 5 9
. 7 9 . . 3 7 .
. 1 2 3 5 . 8 9 6 7
6 2 8 . 1 8 9 . 3 6 5
3 4 . 3 9 7 . 9 7
```

**MEDIUM 52**

```
9 7 . 8 9 6 . 9 7
6 8 . 9 4 7 8 2 . 3 1
8 9 5 7 . . 3 1 4 2
. 7 8 9 . 4 1 2 .
7 8 9 . 2 1 3 . 4 2 1
9 5 . 1 4 2 . 1 3
. 7 1 4 3 . 1 2 4 3
. 2 5 . . 1 2 .
. 1 3 2 5 . 3 5 1 2
1 2 . 8 6 9 . 3 1
2 4 1 . 2 3 7 . 3 1 5
. 2 1 4 . 8 7 9 .
2 1 5 3 . . 5 8 9 7
1 3 . 2 6 7 1 4 . 8 9
4 2 . 4 1 2 . 1 3
```

131

**MEDIUM 53**

**MEDIUM 54**

**MEDIUM 55**

**MEDIUM 56**

**MEDIUM 57**

**MEDIUM 58**

MEDIUM **59**

MEDIUM **60**

MEDIUM **61**

MEDIUM **62**

MEDIUM **63**

MEDIUM **64**

# ANSWERS - MEDIUM

**MEDIUM 65**

**MEDIUM 66**

**MEDIUM 67**

**MEDIUM 68**

**MEDIUM 69**

**MEDIUM 70**

**MEDIUM 71**

**MEDIUM 72**

**MEDIUM 73**

**MEDIUM 74**

**MEDIUM 75**

**MEDIUM 76**

MEDIUM 77

MEDIUM 78

MEDIUM 79

MEDIUM 80

MEDIUM 81

MEDIUM 82

MEDIUM 83

MEDIUM 84

MEDIUM 85

MEDIUM 86

MEDIUM 87

MEDIUM 88

# ANSWERS - MEDIUM

MEDIUM **89**

MEDIUM **90**

HARD **91**

HARD **92**

HARD **93**

HARD **94**

HARD **95**

HARD **96**

HARD **97**

HARD **98**

HARD **99**

HARD **100**